THE COMPLETE ·FURNITURE KIT· CATALOG

Written And Edited By
Jean E. Attebury

·CONTENTS·

Furniture Kit Primer

Priced Any Furniture Lately? 2
Kits: High Quality And Low Price . 3
Furniture Styles 4
Forest To Furniture 6
Tools And Materials ....
Assembly Of Shaker Weaver's Chair .
Assembly Of Two Drawer File .....
Finishes ....
Care ....
Using The Catalogue 1

Furniture Kit Catalogue

Tables 17
Chairs 32
Chests 42
For The Study 54
Clocks 62
Entertainment 66
Wall Systems 71
Shaker Accents 76
Order Forms 78

GARLINGHOUSE

Topeka, Kansas

Isn't it depressing? Not just those high prices, but the idea that it's mostly veneered or laminated plastic and not even solid wood. Right here, among these pages, you'll find just what you've been looking for . . . an inexpensive way to furnish your home with quality, solid-wood furniture for as little as 30% of what you'd pay in your local, retail furniture store.

You don't even have to do any shopping; we've selected more than 150 kits from a number of reputable manufacturers. Everything from clocks, to rockers, to wine racks, to roll-top desks, to Queen Anne low boys is included. We're the clearinghouse, too, so you only complete one form regardless of how many different manufacturers you'd like to order from. We've tried to think of everything, so your only difficulty will be in deciding what to build first.

Browsing through our catalogue section will give you an idea of the variety of furniture now available in kit form, and the prices indicate just how much you can save, but you'll also find that the quality of kit furniture is superior to comparably priced furniture that's turned out by factories. The major portion of the price you pay for the kits is for the wood. You are investing in fine quality wood, not in labor costs or someone's overhead. After all, you're the one who'll be supplying the labor.

You'll know every inch of the furniture you build for yourself and your family. You'll take extra care because it's for your own home. It's that sense of accomplishment and pride that's led man to build for centuries . . . to see the evidence of his labor, his craft. But you don't have to be a gifted artisan or own a completely outfitted workshop to build beautiful, quality furniture from kits. All you need is some time, a little patience and a few, inexpensive tools and materials.

To help you get started building your own furniture from kits, we've developed the **Furniture Kit Primer** to accompany our catalogue. The Primer provides you with the fundamentals of furniture from raw wood, clear through care and maintenance. We've included step-by-step illustrations of assembling two pieces which represent the situations you're most likely to encounter when building your own kits, as well as information regarding styles, woods and finishing techniques to aid your selection. Our **Catalogue** contains a wide variety of pre-cut and simpler, unfinished knocked-down (KD) pieces from which you can choose what is best suited to your taste, skills, needs and budget.

Kit furniture is less expensive and higher in quality than factory-made furniture. You can be sure of quality construction and reliable finishes because you do them yourself. With a little time and effort you can provide furniture of enduring quality that will be a source of pride for years to come.

·KITS: HIGH QUALITY AND LOW PRICE·

Whether building furniture from kits appeals to you because you enjoy woodworking or because your budget won't accommodate furniture store prices doesn't matter. Either way you'll save a lot of money and find a great deal of satisfaction. I know because I've done it myself.

Like most consumers, I demand as much quality as I can possibly afford. I've spent countless hours browsing through furniture stores and flea markets, bidding at auctions and estate sales, and scanning the classified ads in the newspaper. This effort produced a few bargains, but not the combination of quality and savings that I had wanted. When I found that furniture kits were available, I naturally investigated. The price comparisons alone were astonishing.

·1·

Price Comparisons

Golden Oak pieces from the turn of the century are relatively easy to find and are frequently reproduced. A used, oak roll-top desk goes for around $1,000; a restored desk is $1,600; a reproduction is $1,850; but a kit is $549 plus freight. Granted there's a lot of work in a roll-top desk, but I can do a lot of work for $1,300. A matching swivel desk chair kit is $165, restored $258, reproduced $375. The savings is less significant, but then so is the construction time.

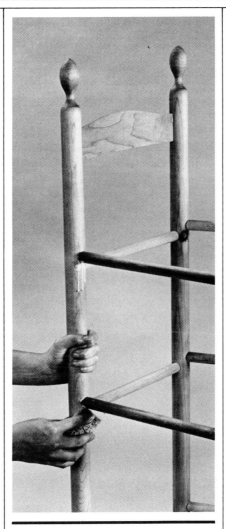

Genuine Queen Anne pieces are virtually impossible to find outside of museums or exclusive antique shops, so the option of restoring them is out. Furniture stores get up to $400 for a tiny, little end table. For another fifty dollars I found a solid cherry kit for a six-drawer writing table. A butler's table, which only takes a couple of hours to construct from a kit priced at $279, sells in the store for $500. That's a little like making over a hundred dollars an hour.

·2·

Solid Construction

The quality of the kits is also remarkable; they are almost exclusively solid wood. No cherry or walnut veneer, but the actual woods themselves. The construction is solid and involves many structural advantages that have been eliminated in today's factory-made furniture. Although some would argue the quality of kits when compared to antiques, I believe that kits are a much better choice. There is no need to restore kits, only to build them all "fresh". All hardware is intact; there are no missing carvings or broken legs; and the old finish doesn't have to be stripped from the, sometimes, brittle wood. In addition, new glues and finishes can increase the durability of the piece, as well as lower the maintenance.

The advantages of building furniture from kits are numerous in terms of savings and quality, but there is also a sense of pride in doing the work yourself. Depending on the complexity of the kit, it might take as little as forty minutes or as much as forty hours to construct your piece, but the satisfaction derived from your project will last as long as the furniture itself.

Good furniture is a blend of beauty and engineering . . . science and art. American furniture is an amalgam of the best of all designs from all over the world. A rich blend of period reproductions, varying influences and practical innovations has produced an exciting array of shapes and designs. Rather than carefully distinguishing among specific styles, Americans tend to compress time into the general categories of traditional and contemporary. What follows is, therefore, not a strictly classical delineation, but an historical description of furniture styles.

·1·

Queen Anne

The American Revolution seemed to signal a change in the world view of just how to label historical periods, and this, in turn, affected the names given to furniture styles. Prior to this era of independence, furniture styles were named for the ruling monarch in the country where the style originated. So it is that the last clearly defined period furniture is named for Queen Anne who ruled England from 1702 until 1714.

The Queen Anne style was in vogue in the Colonies until just before the Revolution. Known for its graceful, curving lines and cabriole legs which commonly terminated in a Dutch or club foot, this style evokes quiet elegance and blends with most other traditional designs. Its graceful lack of ornamentation was easily adapted to the new types of furniture required by the leisure activities enjoyed by the rising middle class. Tea tables, card tables and upholstered sofas made their first appearances in the Queen Anne style.

·2·

Colonial

During the 18th century, which culminated in the Colonies' break with England, increasing numbers of pattern books of furniture were published. This enabled colonial cabinetmakers to copy or adapt European styles in native woods for their American clients. The continuing fame of craftsmen such as England's Thomas Chippendale and America's Duncan Phyfe is due largely to their publication of such books. Colonists from various countries brought pattern books with them and many attempted, in this way, to bring their native cultures and customs with them to the New World.

What is now referred to as Colonial furniture is really a blending of many national, social and political influences. The Pilgrims, the Puritans, the Dutch and the Quakers each had varying customs and philosophies which were reflected in the design of their furniture. While the stoic Pilgrims built furnishings which were plain and heavy, the Dutch cheerfully painted many surfaces with decorative flowers, trees and geometric designs. Fashioned of native pine, maple, hickory, oak, apple and cherry, these village and rural styles were mostly utilitarian and in many instances served dual purposes, so they were designed with a careful eye to strength and durability.

William Penn and George Washington are said to be responsible for the popularity of the Windsor chair in America. Immediately recognizable as Colonial, or Early American, in style, it is distinguished by its bentwood back frame, saddle-shaped seat and legs pegged directly into the chair's seat. Although originally designed by English wheelwrights, Philadelphia cabinetmakers are universally credited with the highly developed design which has remained popular throughout the last two and a half centuries.

·3·
Shaker

Unlike most other American furniture styles, Shaker furniture has remained easily distinguishable from other styles. During the 19th century these "Shaking Quakers" separated themselves from the World (as they termed all outsiders) and developed self-sustaining agrarian communities. They lived spartan lives and devoted themselves to spiritual rather than material goals. The furniture created by their self-trained craftsmen achieved a purity of line equal to their austere philosophy.

The Shakers used rows of pegs placed near their ceilings for hanging storage of chairs, clothing, dried herbs and vegetables and designed hanging shelves and cabinets which made use of this storage system. Many chairs were designed with low backs so that they could be pushed under the table and out of the way when not in use. Chair seats were woven of fabric, usually of two colors, and provided comfort as well as a small decorative touch. They placed casters on the bedsteads so that beds could be moved easily for changing linen or cleaning. Fashioned of local woods such as pine, walnut, maple and fruit woods with almost no ornamentation, Shaker furniture is much admired and copied for its space conserving properties as well as its beauty.

·4·
Turn Of The Century

Machines eventually made furniture more affordable, and transportation systems made it more available to those hardy American pioneers and immigrants who had settled the vast American continent. They had been able to bring few household items with them because of weight considerations, so they poured over the new mail-order catalogues and dreamed of having real furniture. Much of this furniture, particularly the desks and tables, were crafted of oak, but lighter pieces such as china cabinets and dressers employed birds-eye maple, walnut, and sometimes mahogany.

Oak pedestal tables with claw feet, roll-top desks with pigeon holes, pressed back chairs and rockers are all typical of this period. Sturdy office furniture was designed to supply the needs of rapidly growing industry. Filing cabinets and desks with swing out typewriter shelves were devised to assist in the workplace.

Throughout the 20th century furniture styles have become more diverse as both materials and needs have changed. Metals, plastic and foam will continue to mold furniture into shapes as yet unimagined and needs barely conceived, but solid design principles, adapting form to function, will always be in vogue.

The selection of wood is as basic to furniture construction as the determination of style or design. Each type of wood has its own special characteristics and properties, but much is also dependent upon the way the lumber is grown, milled and processed.

All wood is roughly classified as either softwood or hardwood. Softwood comes from evergreen trees such as pine, cedar and fir. Hardwood is produced by trees which lose their leaves annually such as oak, maple and walnut. Of the world's forest resources North America and the Soviet Union contain 83% of the softwood trees, while the tropical regions of Latin America, Africa and Southeast Asia grow 87% of the world's hardwood.

·1·
Lumber

Of the total land area of the United States itself, fully one-third is forest. Although the actual number of hardwood trees exceeds the softwood trees in the United States, the hardwoods require a substantially longer time to grow to a size of any commercial value. Each year 51.7 billion board feet of softwood and only 14.5 billion board feet of hardwood are harvested.

After the trees are harvested, the logs are transported to mills for processing into lumber. Softwoods are dried and then graded at the mill. As they are generally used in construction and not in furniture making, they are evaluated on the basis of uniformity and overall strength. Hardwoods, however, are first graded and then dried.

·2·
Grading

Grading of all lumber is strictly monitored by lumber manufacturing and trade associations. In the case of hardwood the predominant group is the National Hardwood Lumber Association. The basic classifications are determined by rules developed by the U.S. Department of Commerce.

Intended use is the first criterion in grading hardwood. Finished lumber is milled for use as flooring, siding, lath or molding. Dimensional lumber is cut into specific sizes of flat or square stock. Factory lumber is remanufactured into furniture, veneer, paneling or other wood products and is simply sorted by thickness with widths and lengths varying.

The grade of hardwood factory lumber is based on the percentage of unblemished surface and the size of the largest piece which may be cut avoiding all defects. In descending order the grades are Firsts, Seconds (sometimes listed together as Firsts and Seconds, FAS), Selects, No.1 Common, No.2 Common, Sound Wormy, No.3A Common and No.3B Common.

Firsts must be at least 6" × 8' and have 11/12 of the total surface completely free of any defect. The unblemished surface available is measured in cutting units which are 1" × 1' each. Firsts of the minimum size (4 square feet) must contain 44 cutting units (4 sq. ft. × 11) which must be removed as a single piece of wood. Therefore, from the minimum size board of 6" × 8' one perfect piece measuring at least 5 1/2" × 8' would need to be available for that piece of hardwood to be graded Firsts.

Because of the size factor involved, high grade hardwood takes a very long time to grow and is, therefore, quite expensive. The species, especially if it is difficult to obtain, will also influence price. Rarer hardwood specimens graded Firsts or Seconds can easily bring $30,000 per tree.

·3·
Drying

Before wood can be manufactured into furniture or other products, its moisture content must be reduced to that of its intended environment. Simple air drying will reduce the moisture content to about 17%, but this level is only acceptable for exterior construction. Interior use demands moisture levels of 12% or lower, so kiln drying is required.

The moisture content of green hardwoods ranges from 82% in black walnut to 58% in black cherry. At a moisture content of 28% the water within the cell cavities has been removed, but the cell walls still contain bound water which is extracted in the kiln. In order to eliminate most of this water, the kiln operator must slowly raise the temperature, lower the humidity and provide constant air circulation. The water then migrates from the core to the surface where it evaporates.

Careful monitoring of this process is critical so as to avoid stress defects such as warping, checking and case-hardening during this controlled shrinking. In addition to preventing further shrinkage, kiln drying produces wood of greater strength, and lighter weight, as well as better working and finishing surfaces.

·4·
Furniture Woods

Whether it's an oak table that endures spilled cereal or a carefully waxed cherry buffet, the wood in any piece of furniture should be both attractive and durable. While the current variety of finishing stains allows you to "cheat" inexpensive, available pine into expensive, imported mahogany, there's nothing like the real thing.

Pine is the most versatile and available wood. It's the basic structure of most of our homes. This softwood is of a uniform texture and resistant to shrinking, swelling and warping. It works easily, glues readily and accommodates most types of finish. Along with other readily available American woods, it was a basic building material of the early Colonists.

Oak is the most abundant of the native hardwoods and is known for its durability and its natural resistance to moisture. Many old, well-worn pieces that are over a hundred years old survive in homes and in antique stores today. Because of its sturdiness, it was used in furniture which received much wear; therefore, many old pieces have developed deeper colors that can be found in unstained wood. Its bending properties allow craftsmen to readily experiment with shape and form.

Maple is somewhat difficult to locate as lumber but is relatively inexpensive. New England craftsmen took advantage of its inherent strength by using it for chair legs and bracing supports. This strong, hard, fine-textured wood is extremely resistant to abrasion and is used in such practical applications as flooring for bowling alleys, bowling pins and pool cues. Unusual grain patterns such as bird's-eye are highly prized, but are usually only found in veneers. Maple's golden hue and reddish highlights deepen with age.

Walnut furniture is rarely found in stores these days. Although black walnut trees abound in the Midwest, their tendency to grow in fence-rows leaves defects which result in relatively low grade wood. High grade logs are rather unusual and have been known to sell for over $10,000. Darker than most other domestic hardwoods, it is fine-textured, very easily worked and highly resistant to warping and shrinking. English Queen Anne furniture was almost exclusively fashioned of English walnut.

Cherry was the preference of Connecticut cabinetmakers during the Queen Anne period in America. While it's more plentiful than walnut in furniture stores, only the black cherry tree grows to sufficient size for commercial use and that takes about 60 years, so it is relatively scarce. Cherry is known for its beautiful color, texture and glasslike smoothness. With age and exposure to sunlight it reddens and its distinctive luster becomes even deeper. While not so heavy as the other hardwoods, cherry is strong, durable and dimensionally stable.

Mahogany, introduced in the Colonies early in the 18th century, is the most frequently imported furniture wood with Brazil being the largest source. It was used extensively by English designers such as Chippendale, Sheraton and Hepplewhite after being imported by early Spanish explorers. Its fine-grained texture and reddish-brown color produce beautiful furniture, even though it is rather difficult to work because it is somewhat brittle and resists bending. Mahogany, however, is quite durable and dense; these properties account for its extensive use in boat construction.

The kits in the catalogue section offer a choice of wood appropriate to the design and period. Base your selection on the properties which you find most desirable, and the color and texture which you find most attractive.

·1·
Tools

Building furniture from kits requires only simple hand tools and careful assembly. What follows is a list of the tools you'll probably need and the purpose of each. The simpler the kit the fewer the tools, so read the instructions. If you don't have these tools, check with friends and family or invest in what you need. You'll probably find many other uses for them. Having a few tools can save you time and money, not only in building furniture, but also in making simple home repairs.

Woodfile is a wood-sized version of the fingernail file. It should be used to remove any excess material in the area of the joints to insure a perfect fit. In some cases only a little sanding will be necessary, but be very careful not to remove too much.

Rubber mallet will assist in joining pieces such as dovetail joints, legs and spindles. While you may use a hammer and a piece of wood instead, a rubber mallet will offer more protection against denting the wood surface. Many gentle taps are preferable to one good wallop.

Drill, either a hand drill or an electric drill will be needed to start screw holes or to clean out openings for rounded members. Some kits even include the appropriate bits for the job.

Screwdriver, both Phillips and regular screwdrivers, may be used to attach braces, trim, drawer pulls or knobs and drawer glides. They're also very handy for prying off the lids of varnish cans.

Clamps. You simply can't make furniture without clamps. They hold the pieces together while the glue dries, so have plenty. The standard C-clamps and bar clamps (sometimes called pipe clamps) will do most jobs, but you might also want to have a miter clamp which is specifically designed to join corners.

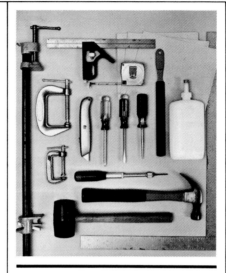

Measurers are deceptively simple devices which aren't usually thought of as tools, but they insure the piece of furniture will be square and level. You wouldn't want to spend many hours on your project only to find that it's lopsided. A tape measure will do most jobs, but you should also invest in a combination square which is a ruler with an attached level. It is truly an all-purpose device.

·2·
Glue

The strength and durability of your furniture is dependent upon the bracing, the joints and the glue which holds them all together. There are three basic glues that are used in furniture construction and each has distinct advantages and disadvantages.

Hide glue is the traditional glue of cabinetmakers and produces an excellent bond and holds up to heavy loads. However, it is susceptible to moisture and becomes very brittle with age. If you've refinished any furniture, you know the condition. It also takes twelve hours to set and then a few more to cure.

Polyvinyl acetate glue, in its most familiar form, is the white glue which comes in squeeze bottles; the modified yellow glue is usually labeled "wood glue" on the bottle and is much better for use in bonding wood. It is moderately moisture resistant and produces structurally sound pieces. After curing the yellow glue remains resilient, so that it adjusts to normal wood movement. Excess should be wiped off with a wet sponge before it dries, as it will not take stain. It sets up in only two or three hours and must be clamped.

Resorcinol resin is probably the best of all the wood bonding materials, but it is also the most difficult to use. It produces a very strong bond which remains slightly resilient when cured. Unlike the other two glues it cures chemically, but is highly water resistant and perfect for outdoor use. In most stores it can be found with waterproof glues used to repair boat seats and the like.

·3·
Sandpaper

Sandpaper is used throughout the process of construction and is the most necessary tool in terms of the finished product. You will need at least three grades. Grades indicate the fineness of the grains which have been glued to the paper. These range from very coarse (12) to superfine (800). For rough work, such as smoothing joints, you will need 60–80 grit paper. For surface work you'll need 120–150 grit paper. For the final finish you'll need 220–280 grit paper. **Never sand across the grain.**

Now that you have all your tools together it's time to get to work. This chair is a good first project. There is no clamping or waiting for glue to dry. It's a simple process of glue and pound. Assembling the chair only took about 30 minutes.

·1·

This kit is quite simple and can be assembled in one afternoon, excluding finishing and seat weaving. Although stain is included, a simple oil finish is enough to bring out the grain. Completely finish the chair prior to weaving the seat to prevent moisture from seeping into the top rails.

·2·

Place a small amount of glue on the tenon of the front rails and in the holes in the front legs.

·3·

Pound the rails into one of the legs, then attach the other leg. Measure to be sure that the unit is square. Using the same gluing and pounding process, attach the side rails to the front legs.

·4·

Once again glue, then pound the front unit into the pre-assembled back unit.

·5·

Check the distance between legs to determine that the diagonal is equal. Adjustments can be made by stringing twine between the two most distant legs and tightening with a long wood scrap. Also check to see that the chair is level. If it wobbles, tap the longest leg on the floor until the wobble is gone.

·6·

Sand and finish as desired before weaving the seat. Thorough instructions and diagrams, as well as inner cushion and tape, are included in each kit.

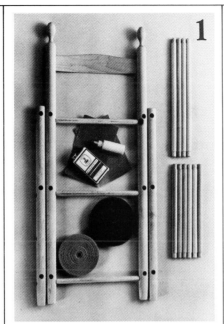

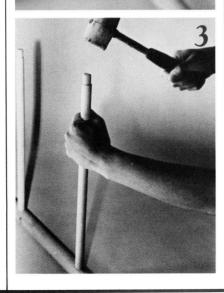

This project is more involved than the chair, but it is not difficult because it goes together in sections. Just progress from section to section and you can complete it in 1½ days. It's best to let the glue dry over night. It's also a good idea to sand the surface of all exterior pieces **before** you glue them all together and then do only a little finish sanding after the piece is assembled.

·1·

This cabinet is prepared in units, so be sure to have all necessary parts at hand before starting. Each piece is stamped with a number corresponding to the instruction diagrams.

·2·

The base unit consists of four horizontal cleats on which the cabinet unit sits, corner cleats for bracing and two panels for added support. The outer sections of the unit are mitered, so miter clamps are necessary.

·3·

Each of the side panels employs grooves to hold the center panels in place. Apply glue to the grooves, slide panels into place, square each unit and clamp.

·4·

The back panels are then inserted into the rear grooves of the side units. The front dividers are glued into the front slots in the side units. Once again, square and clamp.

·5·

Drawer sections are easier to handle when the sides, back and bottom are assembled prior to adding the drawer face. After the unit has dried, add the drawer pulls to the center of the face. Although screws are not mentioned in the instructions, they are better than a clamp for holding the pull in place.

·6·

The base unit can then be glued and screwed to the cabinet.

·7·

Attach the drawer glides to the interior of the cabinet along the cleat and along the lower edge of the drawer unit. Separate instructions are included.

·8·

The drawboard is assembled by gluing and clamping the edges and the face, with its set-in screw, to the large panel. After the unit has dried, add the pull by turning it onto the screw.

·9·

Place the large top unit face down on the floor. Invert the cabinet (without the drawers) on the unit and screw into place.

·10·

Sand the entire surface and finish as desired.

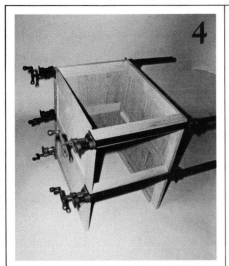

4

7

10

8

5

6

9

Finish coats protect the wood from dirt and moisture and enhance the appearance. Each step should be carefully monitored so that maximum protection and beauty will be achieved. Always read the directions and follow the recommended procedures.

·1·
Preparing the Surface

Sanding produces the final wood surface to which the finishes are applied, so it is very important to produce the smoothest possible surface. Progressive sandings with medium, fine, and superfine grits will produce the best results. Always sand with the grain, **never** across the grain. Continually remove the dust because these particles can cause scratches that won't show up until later. After the final sanding, vacuum the surfaces and dust with a commercial product, such as Endust, which is residue free. Besides making tiny scratches, dust will adhere to the varnish or other finish and cause difficulty in getting a smooth surface.

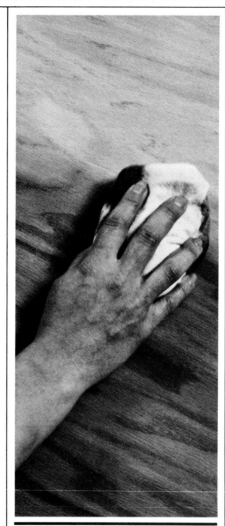

·2·
Staining

Stains are used to alter or enhance the natural color of the wood. With most hardwood this step is quite unnecessary, so you might go on to sealing. It is extremely important to test the stain on a scrap of wood before applying it to the piece of furniture. Plan to use two thin coats rather than one thick one, as this will produce a more even color.

Apply the stain with a cloth or brush both with and across the grain. Wipe off excess after about 15 minutes. Never allow the excess to become dry before removing. After removing excess, allow the piece to dry completely before treating with a second coat or a sealer.

There are three types of stains for wood, and each is generally available in many colors. But each has varying properties you should consider before you make your choice.

Alcohol stains dry very quickly, but they also tend to streak precisely because of this quality. They are, therefore, rather tricky and are usually only recommended for commercial use.

Water stains dry more slowly so you have ample time to distribute them evenly, but they raise the grain of the wood. This requires further sanding before the sealing coat is added. They may also cause warping and swelling due to the amount of moisture they add to the wood, so be careful.

Oil stains are the easiest to use, but they may bleed into the sealer. A penetrating stain is preferable to a pigmented stain, as the latter colors only the surface and tends to obscure the pattern of the grain.

·3·
Sealing

Shellac is the most traditional of the wood finishes, and offers more resistance to dust adhesion than varnish, but it becomes quite brittle with age and produces the tiny cracks which appear on older pieces. It dries in about half an hour unless the weather is humid. Shellac is not very water resistant and may produce white surface rings. It should be applied in two or three coats with sanding between each coat.

Varnish is much more water resistant than shellac, but must be applied in a nearly dust-free environment. It is also slower to dry and should not be applied if the weather is very humid.

Polyurethane finishes are variously classified as varnishes or lacquers. They provide maximum protection against abrasion and moisture, but sometimes peel off in layers. Sanding between coats is not required if applied according to the timing recommended by the manufacturer.

Penetrating resin or oil finishes are most frequently associated with the hand-rubbed look. Elbow grease is what gives them their sheen. Dust does not affect their application as it does varnish, but they are not so water resistant as polyurethane. Three to five coats and lots of buffing with 0000 steel wool between coats will pay off in a fine finish.

·4·
Waxing

Waxing is especially useful in protecting oil finishes, but may also be used effectively on other finishes. This additional layer of protection should be applied, allowed to dry, and buffed to a high gloss.

Well made furniture can last hundreds of years if care is taken to maintain its appearance and structural integrity. Tilting back in chairs, sitting on arms, and tossing keys onto the table by the door will cause damage. Enjoy your furniture, but don't abuse it.

·1·
Protection

Dust is the most pernicious culprit. It causes scratches in finishes that you've spent hours perfecting. Even though it is a loathsome task, dust thoroughly and often using a clean, lint-free cloth and light strokes.

Waxing two or three times a year will create a protective layer over the finish, but be careful not to overdo it. This can actually, as the commercials say, hide the beauty of the wood. If this does occur, just use a little alcohol on a clean cloth to remove this "waxy build-up," then rewax.

Moisture, in the form of humidity, will prevent wood from cracking and splitting. Keep the humidity in your house around 50% if you can. It is also good for preventing static in your carpets.

Sunlight can bleach wood just as it bleaches fabrics. Don't put your prize piece where it will constantly receive direct sunlight.

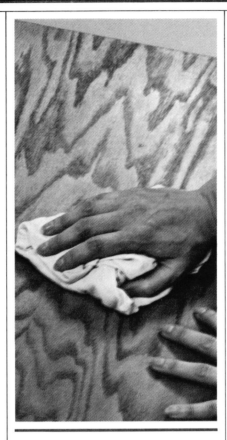

·2·
Trouble-shooting

Small scratches can frequently be remedied by rubbing with a nutmeat such as a walnut or pecan. Larger scratches may be filled with stick shellac of a matching color.

Spills should be removed immediately with a damp sponge, followed by washing with some sudsy water. After drying with a clean cloth, rewax the affected area.

Discolorations may be caused by heat, alcohol or water. Heat marks are usually white, while water causes dark stains. If commercial furniture cleaners don't do the trick, try commercial wood bleach on water marks and undiluted ammonia on heat marks. In either case you will have to spot-finish and rewax after removing the stain.

Small dents can be raised by covering the dent with a damp cloth and then pressing lightly with the tip of a hot iron. The heat should cause the wood to expand to its previous level.

On the following pages you will find more than 150 furniture kits from many different manufacturers, representing varying styles and difficulty. It may be hard to make up your mind. If you've never done any woodworking, it might be a good idea to begin with something relatively simple. The simplicity is not based on the size of a piece, or even the number of pieces, but on the number of different types of operations you have to perform.

Based on my experience, they're all simple. I'm glad that I started on a Shaker chair rather than a block-front chest. By doing the chair first, I gained the confidence that allowed me to get up the nerve to tackle the chest. Much of the time is really waiting for something to dry, so that should be taken into account when figuring how long it will take to complete any project.

Each listing in the catalogue contains the dimensions of the finished piece (D × W × H), the number of pieces and the approximate assembly time. If an item requires only minor assembly and finishing, it is listed as KD or knocked-down.

Some pieces are offered in varying dimensions, different woods or other special features and each of these will carry a different item number. Be sure to check the appropriate item number, as the price will often vary accordingly.

Shipping is handled in several different ways. Freight collect is FC. United Parcel Service collect is UPSC. PP indicates that postage is paid. Some companies list the specific amount of freight and that is included in the listing for the item.

All the kits in this catalogue are guaranteed to be of quality wood and quality craftsmanship. If there is a problem, such as a missing piece, contact the manufacturer directly according to the instructions enclosed in your kit. It happens from time to time, and they'll want to make it right.

If there are any procedures that haven't been covered in the Primer or in your kit's instructions, there are many good books available for do-it-yourselfers in most public libraries. These offer plenty of advice and provide illustrations that are quite helpful.

Try the alternative to high prices and low quality furniture, by building from kits. The savings makes it worth the time, and the satisfaction makes it worth the effort. All in all, it's a great experience that you may get hooked on.

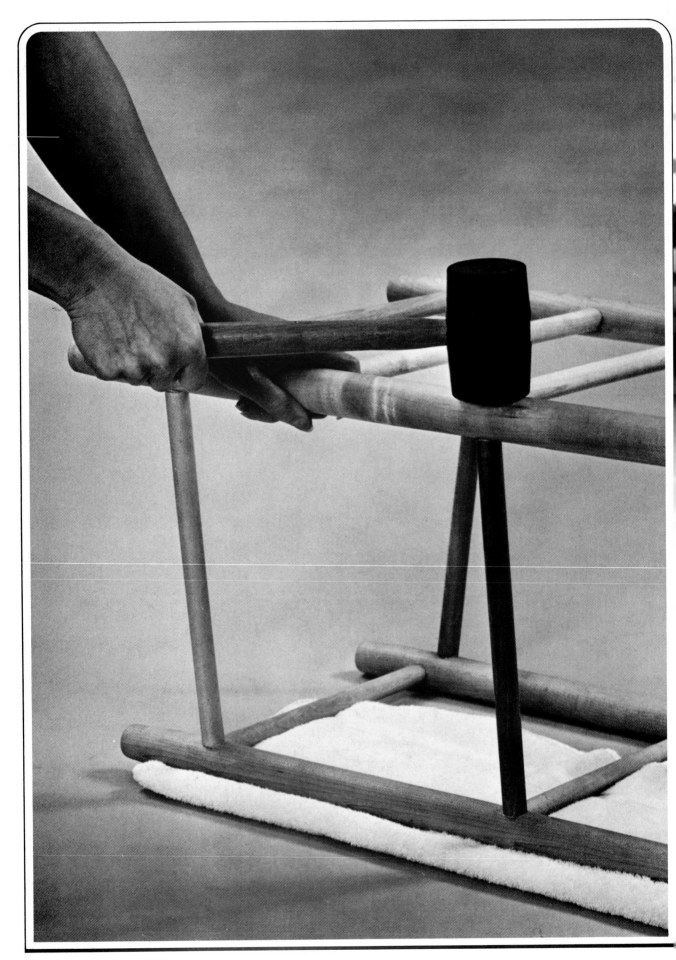

·TABLES·

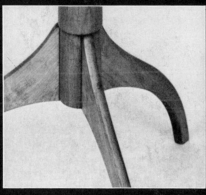

·1·

Choose from two sizes and serpentine or claw foot designs on this rustic pedestal table. Pictured is the 42″ serpentine table with the 12″ leaf which is included with each of these pedestal table kits.

Serpentine Table

Craftsman's Corner
Size: 42″
Pieces: KD
Wood: Oak
Item No.: 1CC121
Price: $349.00
Freight: FC

Size: 48″
Item No.: 1CC123
Price: $389.00
Freight: FC

Claw Foot Table

Size: 42″
Pieces: KD
Wood: Oak
Item No.: 1CC122
Price: $399.00
Freight: FC

Size: 48″
Item No.: 1CC124
Price: $439.00
Freight: FC

·2·

This simple, but elegant trestle table is available in two lengths.

Trestle Table

Design Kit
Size: $36″ \times 72″ \times 28^{1/2}″$
Pieces: KD
Wood: Oak
Item No.: 1DK101
Price: $255.00
Freight: FC

Size: $36″ \times 60″ \times 28^{1/2}″$
Item No.: 1DK102
Price: $234.50
Freight: FC

·3·

This Shaker version of the trestle table features a pine table top and maple legs and stretchers. Although available in four lengths, each table is 33″ deep and 29″ high. Each kit contains 6 pieces and takes four hours to assemble.

60″ Trestle Table
Shaker Workshops
Item No.: 1SW117
Price: $310.00
Freight: FC

72″ Trestle Table
Item No.: 1SW118
Price: $340.00
Freight: FC

84″ Trestle Table
Item No.: 1SW119
Price: $370.00
Freight: FC

96″ Trestle Table
Item No.: 1SW120
Price: $400.00
Freight: FC

·4·

Bridge Luncheon Table
Ellsworth Cabinet, Inc.
Size: 36″ × 36″ × 28″
(Closed: 20½″ × 36″ × 28″)
Pieces: KD
Wood: Cherry
Item No.: 1EW100
Price: $257.50
Freight: FC

·1·

Lamp Table
American Forest Products
Size: 20″ × 24⅞″ × 21″
Pieces: 5
Time: 1/4 hour
Wood: Pine
Item No.: 1AF116
Price: $71.25
Freight: $9.25

·2·

Chow Table
American Forest Products
Size: 18″ × 19¾″ × 16″
Pieces: 5
Time: 1/4 hour
Wood: Pine
Item No.: 1AF117
Price: $53.75
Freight: $7.00

·3·

Lamp Table
Ellsworth Cabinet, Inc.
Size: 21″ × 26″ × 21″
Pieces: KD
Wood: Cherry
Item No.: 1EW107
Price: $194.25
Freight: UPSC

·4·

Console Table
Ellsworth Cabinet, Inc.
Size: 11½″ × 22½″ × 29″
Pieces: KD
Wood: Cherry
Item No.: 1EW120
Price: $177.50
Freight: UPSC

·5·

End Table

Ellsworth Cabinet, Inc.
Size: 21″ × 21″ × 21″
Pieces: KD
Wood: Cherry
Item No.: 1EW123
Price: $163.50
Freight: UPSC

·6·

Oblong End Table

Ellsworth Cabinet, Inc.
Size: 20″ × 26″ × 21″
Pieces: KD
Wood: Cherry
Item No.: 1EW115
Price: $138.50
Freight: UPSC

·7·

Bunching Tables

Ellsworth Cabinet, Inc.
Size: 21″ × 21″ × 16″
Pieces: KD
Wood: Cherry
Item No.: 1EW109
Price: $154.25 each
Freight: UPSC

·8·

Lamp Table

Ellsworth Cabinet, Inc.
Size: 18″ × 26″ × 24″
Pieces: KD
Wood: Cherry
Item No.: 1EW104
Price: $125.75
Freight: UPSC

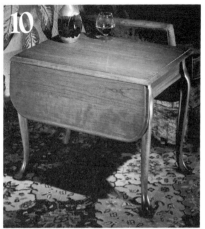

·9·

Cat's Paw Pembroke
Ellsworth Cabinet, Inc.
Size: 36″ × 26″ × 24″
(Closed: 20″ × 26″ × 24″)
Pieces: KD
Wood: Cherry
Item No.: 1EW136
Price: $179.50
Freight: UPSC

·10·

Queen Anne Pembroke
Ellsworth Cabinet, Inc.
Size: 36″ × 26″ × 21″
(Closed: 20″ × 26″ × 21″)
Pieces: KD
Wood: Cherry
Item No.: 1EW108
Price: $202.00
Freight: UPSC

·11·

Oval Pembroke Table
Ellsworth Cabinet, Inc.
Size: 33″ × 26″ × 24″
(Closed: 18″ × 26″ × 24″)
Pieces: KD
Wood: Cherry
Item No.: 1EW127
Price: $199.50
Freight: UPSC

·12·

Butterfly Table
Ellsworth Cabinet, Inc.
Size: 21″ × 26″ × 24″
Pieces: KD
Wood: Cherry
Item No.: 1EW125
Price: $171.00
Freight: UPSC

·13·

Drawer End Table
Ellsworth Cabinet, Inc.
Size: 18″ × 23″ × 20½″
Pieces: KD
Wood: Cherry
Item No.: 1EW102
Price: $199.50
Freight: UPSC

·14·

Lamp Table with Drawer
Ellsworth Cabinet, Inc.
Size: 21″ × 21″ × 24″
Pieces: KD
Wood: Cherry
Item No.: 1EW106
Price: $149.50
Freight: UPSC

·15·

Lamp Table
Ellsworth Cabinet, Inc.
Size: 21″ × 21″ × 21″
Pieces: KD
Wood: Cherry
Item No.: 1EW129
Price: $177.50
Freight: UPSC

·1·
Coffee Table
American Forest Products
Size: 20″ × 47″ × 16″
Pieces: 5
Time: 1/4 hour
Wood: Pine
Item No.: 1AF115
Price: $87.50
Freight: $12.50

·2·
Cocktail Table
Ellsworth Cabinet, Inc.
Size: 20″ × 46″ × 16″
Pieces: KD
Wood: Cherry
Item No.: 1EW116
Price: $197.50
Freight: FC

·3·
Design Kit Corner Table
Size: $30^3/4''$ × $30^3/4''$ × 16″
Pieces: KD
Wood: Oak
Item No.: 1DK104
Price: $118.25
Freight: UPSC

·4·
Design Kit Coffee Table
Size: 36″ × 36″ × 16″
Pieces: KD
Wood: Oak
Item No.: 1DK103
Price: $137.00
Freight: FC

(Not Shown)
Design Kit Side Table
Size: $26^3/4''$ × $26^3/4''$ × 16″
Pieces: KD
Wood: Oak
Item No.: 1DK105
Price: $87.00
Freight: UPSC

·5·

Drop Leaf Cocktail Table

Ellsworth Cabinet, Inc.
Size: 30″ × 44″ × 16″
(Closed: 19″ × 44″ × 16″)
Pieces: KD
Wood: Cherry
Item No.: 1EW117
Price: $226.25
Freight: FC

·6·

Cat's Paw Cocktail Table

Ellworth Cabinet, Inc.
Size: 21″ × 48″ × 16″
Pieces: KD
Wood: Cherry
Item No.: 1EW137
Price: $162.75
Freight: FC

·7·

Cocktail Table

Ellsworth Cabinet, Inc.
Size: 21″ × 48″ × 16″
Pieces: KD
Wood: Cherry
Item No.: 1EW126
Price: $164.25
Freight: FC

·8·

Oval Cocktail Table

Ellsworth Cabinet, Inc.
Size: 25″ × 43″ × 16″
Pieces: KD
Wood: Cherry
Item No.: 1EW121
Price: $175.75
Freight: FC

·1·

Buffet Table
Design Kit
Size: 18″ × 60″ × 28½″
Pieces: KD
Wood: Oak
Item No.: 1DK100
Price: $206.25
Freight: FC

·2·

Queen Anne Sofa Table
Ellsworth Cabinet, Inc.
Size: 14″ × 44″ × 28″
Pieces: KD
Wood: Cherry
Item No.: 1EW110
Price: $207.50
Freight: UPSC

·3·

Traditional Sofa Table
Ellsworth Cabinet, Inc.
Size: 14″ × 44″ × 28″
Pieces: KD
Wood: Cherry
Item No.: 1EW101
Price: $222.00
Freight: UPSC

·4·

Queen Anne Side Table
Ellsworth Cabinet, Inc.
Size: 18″ × 38″ × 30″
Pieces: KD
Wood: Cherry
Item No.: 1EW131
Price: $255.75
Freight: FC

This elegant table features solid brass drawer pulls which are included in the kit.

·1·

Backgammon Table
Ellsworth Cabinet, Inc.
Size: 26½" × 26½" × 28"
Pieces: KD
Wood: Cherry
Item No.: 1EW128
Price: $299.50
Freight: UPSC

This table is distinguished by its walnut, maple and mahogany inlay of the playing surface.

·2·

Lift-Off Tray Table
Ellsworth Cabinet, Inc.
Size: 13" × 21½" × 22"
Pieces: KD
Wood: Cherry
Item No.: 1EW130
Price: $212.25
Freight: UPSC

Two pieces in one create this functional, yet elegant serving table.

·3·

Chess Table
Ellsworth Cabinet, Inc.
Size: 25" × 25" × 28"
Pieces: KD
Wood: Cherry
Item No.: 1EW111
Price: $216.25
Freight: UPSC

The perfect display for your best chess set with maple and walnut inlay.

·1·

Pie Crust Tilt Top
Ellsworth Cabinet, Inc.
Size: 23″ × 25″
Pieces: KD
Wood: Cherry
Item No.: 1EW103
Price: $118.50
Freight: UPSC

·2·

Book Stand
Ellsworth Cabinet, Inc.
Size: 14″ × 16″ × 40″
Pieces: KD
Wood: Cherry
Item No.: 1EW112
Price: $110.50
Freight: UPSC

Display your finest heirloom books or Bible on this lustrous cherry stand.

·3·

Kettle Stand
Ellsworth Cabinet, Inc.
Size: 12″ × 24″
Pieces: KD
Wood: Cherry
Item No.: 1EW113
Price: $64.50
Freight: UPSC

·4·

Shaker Fern Stand
Ellsworth Cabinet, Inc.
Size: 12″ × 36″
Pieces: KD
Wood: Cherry
Item No.: 1EW114
Price: $68.50
Freight: UPSC

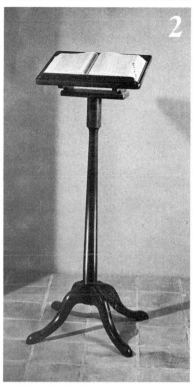

·5·

Hooded Candle Stand
Ellsworth Cabinet, Inc.
Size: 15″ × 11″ × 47″
Pieces: KD
Wood: Cherry
Item No.: 1EW119
Price: $95.00
Freight: UPSC

·6·

Round Candle Stand
Shaker Workshops
Size: 17½″ × 25½″
Pieces: 6
Time: 1 hour
Wood: Maple
Item No.: 1SW109
Price: $47.50
Freight: $4.00

·7·

Candle Stand
Shaker Workshops
Size: 17¾″ × 20″ × 25½″
Pieces: 6
Time: 1 hour
Wood: Maple
Item No.: 1SW110
Price: $50.00
Freight: $4.50

·8·

Wash Basin Stand
Craftsman's Corner
Size: 16″ × 22″ × 32″
Pieces: 20
Time: 4 hours
Wood: Oak
Item No.: 1CC131
Price: $99.95
Freight: $8.50

·9·

Round Table
Ellsworth Cabinet, Inc.
Size: 20″ × 25″
Pieces: KD
Wood: Cherry
Item No.: 1EW118
Price: $83.25
Freight: UPSC

·10·

Plant Stand
Craftsman's Corner
Size: 12³/4″ × 20³/4″
Pieces: 26
Time: 1 hour
Wood: Oak
Item No.: 1CC110
Price: $24.95
Freight: $3.75

·11·

Demitasse Table
Ellsworth Cabinet, Inc.
Size: 15″ × 15″ × 24″
Pieces: KD
Wood: Cherry
Item No.: 1EW105
Price: $69.50
Freight: UPSC

·CHAIRS·

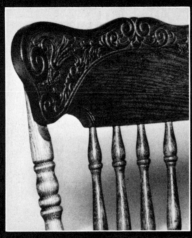

·1·

Frisco Arm Chair
Craftsman's Corner
Size: 17³/₁₆″ × 21″ × 42″
Pieces: Assembled, unfinished
Wood: Oak
Item No.: 1CC120
Price: $159.00
Freight: FC

·2·

Elder's Chair
Shaker Workshops
Size: 18″ × 22″ × 51¹/₂″
Pieces: 24
Time: 4 hours
Wood: Maple
Item No.: 1SW104
Price: $112.50
Freight: $5.50

Design Kit offers its oak Lounge Chair with 3/8″ oak slats, with 1″ urethane cushions covered in natura fabric, or with a sling of natural cowhide. Only minor assembly is needed.

·3·

Lounge Chair with Slats
Size: 26″ × 27¹/₂″ × 28³/₄″
Item No.: 1DK106
Price: $84.00
Freight: UPSC

Lounge Chair with Cloth Cushions
Size: 26″ × 27¹/₂″ × 28³/₄″
Item No.: 1DK107
Price: $92.50
Freight: UPSC

Lounge Chair with Leather Sling
Size: 26″ × 27¹/₂″ × 29³/₄″
Item No.: 1DK108
Price: $235.25
Freight: UPSC

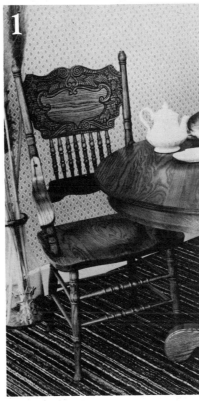

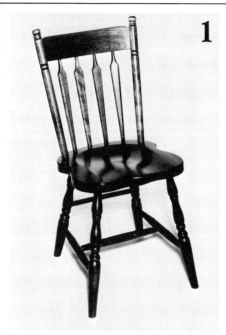

·1·

Arrowback Chair

Zimmerman Chair Shop
Size: 17″ × 18″ × 36″
Pieces: 16
Time: 2½ hours
Wood: Oak
Item No.: 1ZC102
Price: $110.00
Freight: $6.60

·2·

Bowback Windsor Chair

Zimmerman Chair Shop
Size: 17″ × 18″ × 37½″
Pieces: 17
Time: 3 hours
Wood: Oak
Item No.: 1ZC103
Price: $115.00
Freight: $6.90

·3·

Low Back Chair

Shaker Workshops
Size: 14″ × 18¾″ × 27″
Pieces: 17
Time: 3 hours
Wood: Maple
Item No.: 1SW101
Price: $60.00
Freight: $3.75

Designed by the Shakers to slide under the table when not in use, this chair is an example of their space-conscious design.

·4·

Straight Chair

Shaker Workshops
Size: 14″ × 18¾″ × 42″
Pieces: 18
Time: 3 hours
Wood: Maple
Item No.: 1SW102
Price: $70.00
Freight: $4.00

·5·

Frisco Chair
Craftsman's Corner
Size: 17³/₁₆″ × 21″ × 42″
Pieces: Assembled, unfinished
Wood: Oak
Item No.: 1CC119
Price: 2 @ $219.95
Freight: FC

·6·

Hoop Back Chair
Craftsman's Corner
Size: 15³/₄″ × 18¹/₂″ × 35¹/₂″
Pieces: KD
Wood: Oak
Item No.: 1CC101
Price: $94.95
Freight: $12.00

·7·

Embossed Back Chair
Zimmerman Chair Shop
Size: 17″ × 18″ × 38¹/₂″
Pieces: 21
Time: 2¹/₂ hours
Wood: Oak
Item No.: 1ZC100
Price: $120.00
Freight: $7.20

·8·

Pressback Chair with Cane Seat
Craftsman's Corner
Size: 16″ × 21″ × 39″
Pieces: Assembled, unfinished
Wood: Oak
Item No.: 1CC225
Price: 2 @ $189.95
Freight: FC

Also available with a solid, saddle seat.

Pressback Chair with Saddle Seat
Item No.: 1CC125
Price: 2 @ $189.95
Freight: FC

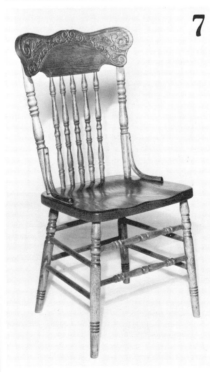

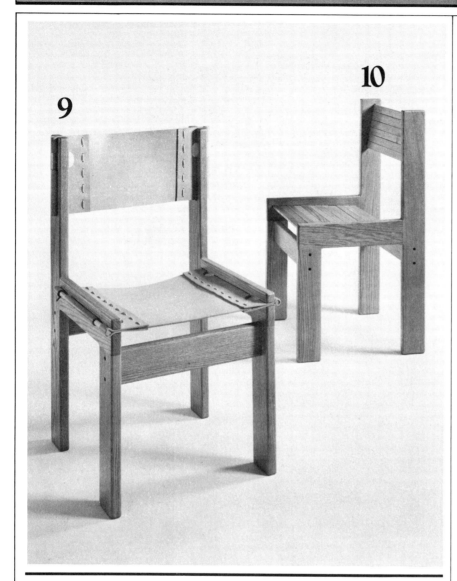

·9·

Leather Sling Chair
Design Kit
Size: 19³/₈″ × 18³/₄″ × 34³/₄″
Pieces: KD
Wood: Oak
Item No.: 1DK115
Price: $91.50
Freight: UPSC

If you prefer, this same chair may be ordered with a canvas sling instead of the leather sling that is pictured.

Canvas Sling Chair
Item No.: 1DK117
Price: $62.75
Freight: UPSC

·10·

Oak Slat Chair
Design Kit
Size: 19³/₈″ × 18³/₄″ × 34³/₄″
Pieces: KD
Wood: Oak
Item No.: 1DK116
Price: $60.50
Freight: UPSC

·1·

Mount Lebanon Settee
Shaker Workshops
Size: 19″ × 43½″ × 37½″
Pieces: 23
Time: 9 hours
Wood: Maple
Item No.: 1SW116
Price: $200.00
Freight: $7.55

Described as "the rarest of all Shaker furniture," this double arm-chair was originally made in the South Family chair shop at Mt. Lebanon, New York toward the end of the 19th century. Only about six of the originals have survived.

·2·

Couch Frame
Design Kit
Size: 31″ × 76″ × 31″
Pieces: KD
Wood: Oak
Item No.: 1DK113
Price: $178.25
Freight: UPSC

Cushions are not included with this kit.

·3·

Park Bench
Craftsman's Corner
Size: 21½″ × 48″ × 26½″
Pieces: 7
Time: 1 hour
Wood: Hardwood
Item No.: 1CC106
Price: $89.95
Freight: $17.00

Complete kit includes solid, rustproof, cast iron ends, pre-drilled hardwood bench and back slats, complete hardware and instructions.

·1·
Child's Rocker
Shaker Workshops
Size: 11½″ × 15″ × 29″
Pieces: 24
Time: 5 hours
Wood: Maple
Item No.: 1SW100
Price: $63.75
Freight: $3.25

·2·
Child's Chair
Shaker Workshops
Size: 11½″ × 15″ × 28″
Pieces: 18
Time: 3 hours
Wood: Maple
Item No.: 1SW123
Price: $47.50
Freight: $3.25

·3·
Child's Arm Chair
Shaker Workshops
Size: 11½″ × 15″ × 28″
Pieces: 22
Time: 3 hours
Wood: Maple
Item No.: 1SW122
Price: $55.00
Freight: $3.25

·4·
Youth Chair
Shaker Workshops
Size: 11½″ × 15″ × 34½″
(Seat is 21″ high)
Pieces: 19
Time: 3 hours
Wood: Maple
Item No.: 1SW115
Price: $70.00
Freight: $3.45

·1·

Shawl Back Rocker

Shaker Workshops
Size: 19″ × 23″ × 42″
Pieces: 26
Time: 5 hours
Wood: Maple
Item No.: 1SW106
Price: $127.50
Freight: $5.50

·2·

Slat Back Rocker

Shaker Workshops
Size: 19″ × 23″ × 42″
Pieces: 26
Time: 5 hours
Wood: Maple
Item No.: 1SW121
Price: $122.50
Freight: $5.50

·3·

Tape Back Rocker

Shaker Workshops
Size: 19″ × 23″ × 42″
Pieces: 24
Time: 6 hours
Wood: Maple
Item No.: 1SW105
Price: $132.50
Freight: $5.75

This Tape Back Rocker may also be ordered with a shawl rail as shown in item number 1SW106 on this page.

Tape Back Rocker with Shawl Rail

Shaker Workshops
Size: 19″ × 23″ × 42″
Pieces: 25
Time: 6 hours
Wood: Maple
Item No.: 1SW126
Price: $137.50
Freight: $5.75

·1·

Foot Stool
Shaker Workshops
Size: 10″ × 13″ × 10″
Pieces: 12
Time: 2 hours
Wood: Maple
Item No.: 1SW108
Price: $30.00
Freight: $2.70

·2·

Weaver's Chair
Shaker Workshops
Size: 14″ × 18¾″ × 39″
Pieces: 16
Time: 3 hours
Wood: Maple
Item No.: 1SW103
Price: $65.00
Freight: $4.25

This Shaker design with its 26″ seat is perfect for the kitchen counter or the bar area.

·3·

Folding Hobby Seat
Smith Wood Products
Size: 10″ × 14″ × 14″
Pieces: 21
Time: ½ hour
Wood: Oak
Item No.: 1BG100
Price: $19.95
Freight: $3.50

·4·

Spinning Stool
Shaker Workshops
Size: 14″ × 18″ × 15½″
Pieces: 16
Time: 3 hours
Wood: Maple
Item No.: 1SW107
Price: $40.00
Freight: $3.25

These versatile pieces may be used as either stools or small tables and complement any style of furniture.

·5·

Bar Stool
Design Kit
Size: 16″ × 16″ × 30″
Pieces: KD
Wood: Oak
Item No.: 1DK109
Price: $46.75
Freight: UPSC

·6·

Kitchen Stool
Design Kit
Size: 16″ × 16″ × 24″
Pieces: KD
Wood: Oak
Item No.: 1DK110
Price: $44.25
Freight: UPSC

·7·

Dining Stool
Design Kit
Size: 16″ × 16″ × 18″
Pieces: KD
Wood: Oak
Item No.: 1DK111
Price: $38.50
Freight: UPSC

·8·

Foot Stool
Design Kit
Size: 16″ × 16″ × 12″
Pieces: KD
Wood: Oak
Item No.: 1DK112
Price: $34.00
Freight: UPSC

·CHESTS·

·1·

Classic Six-Drawer Chest
Craftsman's Corner
Size: $19^1/2'' \times 34'' \times 44^1/2''$
Pieces: 70
Time: 11 hours
Wood: Oak
Item No.: 1CC127
Price: $249.00
Freight: $34.00

·2·

Classic Night Stand
Craftsman's Corner
Size: $16'' \times 20'' \times 25^3/4''$
Pieces: 30
Time: 5 hours
Wood: Oak
Item No.: 1CC128
Price: $99.95
Freight: $14.00

·3·

Credenza with Mirror Frame
Craftsman's Corner
Size: $10^1/2'' \times 28'' \times 28''$
(Frame: $19'' \times 36''$)
Pieces: 70
Time: 5 hours
Wood: Oak
Item No.: 1CC108
Price: $149.95
Freight: $18.00

Metal mesh screens for the credenza are included, but the mirror is not.

·4·

Chairside Chest
Ellsworth Cabinet, Inc.
Size: $13'' \times 21^1/2'' \times 22''$
Pieces: KD
Wood: Cherry
Item No.: 1EW122
Price: $292.00
Freight: UPSC

·5·

Four-Drawer Chest
American Forest Products
Size: $16^5/_{16}''$ × $30^9/_{16}''$ × $39^1/_{16}''$
Pieces: 35
Time: $1^1/_2$ hours
Wood: Pine
Item No.: 1AF101
Price: $143.00
Freight: FC

·6·

Queen Anne Low-Boy
Ellsworth Cabinet, Inc.
Size: 18″ × 23″ × 30″
Pieces: KD
Wood: Cherry
Item No.: 1EW124
Price: $269.75
Freight: FC

Solid brass drawer pulls produced from antique molds are included with the kit.

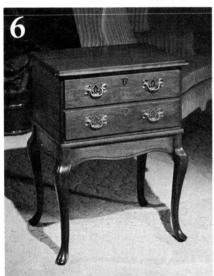

·7·

All Purpose Chest
American Forest Products
Size: $16^5/_{16}''$ × $21^3/_8''$ × $26^3/_{16}''$
Pieces: 29
Time: $1^1/_4$ hours
Wood: Pine
Item No.: 1AF102
Price: $86.00
Freight: $12.50

·8·

Armoire
American Forest Products
Size: $16^5/_{16}'' \times 30^9/_{16}'' \times 54^3/_{16}''$
Pieces: 60
Time: 5 hours
Wood: Pine
Item No.: 1AF106
Price: $217.75
Freight: FC

·9·

Lingerie Chest
American Forest Products
Size: $16^5/_{16}'' \times 21^3/_8'' \times 54^3/_{16}''$
Pieces: 64
Time: $2^1/_2$ hours
Wood: Pine
Item No.: 1AF109
Price: $166.00
Freight: FC

·10·

Seven-Drawer Dresser
American Forest Products
Size: $16^5/_{16}'' \times 58^1/_4'' \times 30^{15}/_{16}''$
Pieces: 68
Time: $3^1/_2$ hours
Wood: Pine
Item No.: 1AF100
Price: $199.00
Freight: FC

·1·

Dry Sink
Craftsman's Corner
Size: 17¼″ × 32½″ × 36″
Pieces: 57
Time: 6 hours
Wood: Oak
Item No.: 1CC114
Price: $189.95
Freight: $19.00

·2·

Two-Door Cabinet
American Forest Products
Size: 16⁵/₁₆″ × 28¹¹/₁₆″ × 21⁷/₈″
Pieces: 17
Time: 1 hour
Wood: Pine
Item No.: 1AF104
Price: $74.50
Freight: $9.50

·3·

Authentic Lyreback Commode
Craftsman's Corner
Size: 18″ × 28½″ × 56½″
Pieces: 66
Time: 9 hours
Wood: Oak
Item No.: 1CC129
Price: $199.00
Freight: $22.00

·1·

Lift Top Chest

American Forest Products
Size: $16^{5}/_{16}'' \times 36'' \times 18^{7}/_{8}''$
Pieces: 19
Time: 1 hour
Wood: Pine
Item No.: 1AF107
Price: $81.00
Freight: $9.75

·2·

Steamer Trunk

Craftsman's Corner
Size: $16^{3}/_{8}'' \times 32'' \times 16^{1}/_{2}''$
Pieces: 44
Time: 6 hours
Wood: Oak
Item No.: 1CC116
Price: $199.95
Freight: $18.00

This cedar-lined chest is constructed of triple half-inch veneer consisting of an outer layer of oak, then plywood and cedar on the interior. The inner tray is cedar and the leather handles and all hardware are included.

1

Hutch

Craftsman's Corner
Size: 18″ × 38″ × 79″
(Base: 18″ × 38″ × 34″)
(Top: 12″ × 36″ × 45″)
Pieces: 121
Time: 16 hours
Wood: Oak
Item No.: 1CC105
Price: $499.00
Freight: FC

Display your precious dishes or other prized knick-knacks in this commanding hutch which includes its own leaded glass panels. Hand-cut clear glass sections are accented with diamonds of amber glass, all hand-soldered into genuine lead came. Each section is complete and ready to install in the door frames. All of the reproduced, period hardware with its burnished finish is included. Shelves in the top sections are adjustable. The wood is oak and oak-veneer panels for lighter weight.

·2·

This Victorian Curio China Cabinet can be selected with mahogany back panel or a mirrored back panel which gives added depth to your collected treasures. Both cabinets are fully assembled with the exception of the attachment of the top pedement. Each features four, ¼″ thick plate glass shelves which are top-lighted. Curved glass door and side panels are enhanced by brass trim and a brass lock and key are also included.

Mahogany-Back Curio China Cabinet

Craftsman's Corner
Size: 36″ wide × 62″ high
Pieces: KD
Wood: Oak
Item No.: 1CC118
Price: $419.00
Freight: FC

Mirror-Back Curio China Cabinet

Craftsman's Corner
Size: 36″ wide × 62″ high
Pieces: KD
Wood: Oak
Item No.: 1CC126
Price: $469.99
Freight: FC

·3·

Crown Top Curio
Sechtem's Furniture Co.
Size: $6^1/2'' \times 21^1/2'' \times 28''$
Pieces: 85
Time: 3 hours
Wood: Pine
Item No.: 1SF100
Price: $104.00
Freight: $10.40

Curved glass and all hardware are included in the kit.

·4·

The Spindle Top Curio is available in four different woods and includes all curved glass and hardware.

Spindle Top Curio
Sechtem's Furniture Co.
Size: $6^1/2'' \times 21^1/2'' \times 28^1/2''$
Pieces: 97
Time: 4 hours
Wood: Pine
Item No.: 1SF101
Price: $95.00
Freight: $9.50

Wood: Oak
Item No.: 1SF201
Price: $116.00
Freight: $11.60

Wood: Cherry
Item No.: 1SF301
Price: $120.00
Freight: $12.00

Wood: Walnut
Item No.: 1SF401
Price: $125.00
Freight: $12.50

Select the Antique Screw Cabinet with screw sizes burned into each drawer or decorate these octagonal beauties with your own designs. Each kit includes a swivel base. Knobs are not included so that you are free to make your own selection from those offered on page 53.

·1·

72-Drawer Antique Screw Cabinet

Sechtem's Furniture Co.
Size: 21⅝″ × 30″
Pieces: 560
Time: 20 hours
Wood: Pine
Item No.: 1SF102
Price: $389.00
Freight: $38.90

·2·

40-Drawer Screw Cabinet

Size: 21⅝″ × 17½″
Pieces: 336
Time: 14 hours
Wood: Pine
Item No.: 1SF104
Price: $215.00
Freight: $21.50

Each additional 16 drawers adds 5¾″ to the height, 112 pieces and 2 hours of assembly time.

·3·

56-Drawer Screw Cabinet

Item No.: 1SF103
Price: $255.00
Freight: $25.50

·4·

72-Drawer Screw Cabinet

Item No.: 1SF109
Price: $295.00
Freight: $29.50

Hexagonal Tiki Cabinets can be arranged in a number of interesting ways. Each kit includes a swivel base. Knobs are not included, so choose from those pictured on page 53.

·5·

6-Drawer Tiki Cabinet
Sechtem's Furniture Co.
Size: 12″ × 4½″
Pieces: 66
Time: 3 hours
Wood: Pine
Item No.: 1SF105
Price: $36.00
Freight: $3.60

Each additional layer of six drawers adds 2¼″ of height, 54 pieces and 30 minutes of assembly time.

·6·

12-Drawer Tiki Cabinet
Item No.: 1SF106
Price: $43.00
Freight: $4.30

·7·

18-Drawer Tiki Cabinet
Item No.: 1SF107
Price: $49.00
Freight: $4.90

·8·

24-Drawer Tiki Cabinet
Item No.: 1SF108
Price: $56.00
Freight: $5.60

·1·

Porcelain Knobs

Sechtem's Furniture Co.
Size: ³/₄″ diameter by ³/₄″ long
Item No.: 1SF110
Price: $0.89 each
Freight: FC

·2·

Pine Knobs

Sechtem's Furniture Co.
Size: ³/₄″ diameter by ⁵/₈″ long
Item No.: 1SF111
Price: $0.15 each
Freight: FC

Shaker Workshops offers its maple knobs in three diameters and quantities of ten or fifty. The ³/₄″ knobs have a ³/₈″ tenon; the other knobs have ¹/₂″ tenons. All freight for these knobs is postage paid.

·3·

³/₄″ Shaker Knobs

Item No.: 1SW127
Price: 10 @ $2.80

Item No.: 1SW128
Price: 50 @ $8.40

·4·

1¹/₄″ Shaker Knobs

Item No.: 1SW129
Price: 10 @ $3.75

Item No.: 1SW130
Price: 50 @ $13.00

·5·

1³/₄″ Shaker Knobs

Item No.: 1SW131
Price: 10 @ $4.65

Item No.: 1SW132
Price: 50 @ $17.05

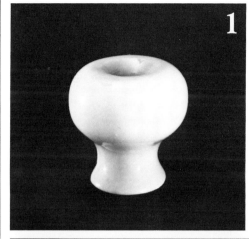

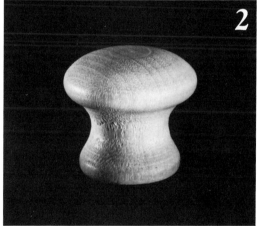

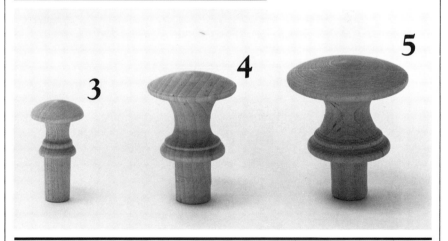

·FOR THE STUDY·

All fittings and pulls for both of these lovely cherry desks are solid brass produced from antique molds.

·1·

Gentleman's Writing Table

Ellsworth Cabinet, Inc.
Size: 20″ × 44″ × 30½″
Pieces: KD
Wood: Cherry
Item No.: 1EW132
Price: $316.75
Freight: FC

Matching Bench

Ellsworth Cabinet, Inc.
Size: 15″ × 23″ × 18″
Pieces: KD
Wood: Cherry
Item No.: 1EW133
Price: $145.25
Freight: UPSC

·2·

Lady's Queen Anne Desk

Ellsworth Cabinet, Inc.
Size: 18″ × 38″ × 30″
Pieces: KD
Wood: Cherry
Item No.: 1EW134
Price: $368.00
Freight: FC

Matching Bench

Ellsworth Cabinet, Inc.
Size: 18″ × 23″ × 19″
Pieces: KD
Wood: Cherry
Item No.: 1EW135
Price: $113.50
Freight: UPSC

·3·
Roll Top Desk
American Forest Products
Size: 22″ × 55″ × 45¹/₁₆″
Pieces: 87
Time: 7 hours
Wood: Pine
Item No.: 1AF108
Price: $349.50
Freight: FC

·4·
Master Piece Desk
American Forest Products
Size: 19″ × 41″ × 31¹³/₁₆″
Pieces: 38
Time: 2¼ hours
Wood: Pine
Item No.: 1AF103
Price: $149.25
Freight: FC

·5·

Four-Drawer Roll Top Desk

American Forest Products
Size: 19¼″ × 41″ × 45⅛″
Pieces: 54
Time: 5½ hours
Wood: Pine
Item No.: 1AF111
Price: $245.25
Freight: FC

·6·

Drop Lid Secretary Desk

American Forest Products
Size: 15⅝″ × 30⁹/₁₆″ × 44⅙″
Pieces: 51
Time: 3½ hours
Wood: Pine
Item No.: 1AF110
Price: $222.25
Freight: FC

·7·

Elegant Roll Top Desk
Craftsman's Corner
Size: 22″ × 41″ × 43¾″
Pieces: 93
Time: 8 hours
Wood: Oak
Item No.: 1CC100
Price: $339.95
Freight: $34.00

Two good-sized drawers under the work surface are ample for stationery or household records. Each leg is hand-turned from a solid oak blank. The tambour roll top is pre-assembled, ready to install.

·8·

Space Saver Roll Top Desk
Craftsman's Corner
Size: 26″ × 41″ × 45″
Pieces: 150
Time: 25 hours
Wood: Oak
Item No.: 1CC107
Price: $389.00
Freight: FC

Lots of room plus pencil trays, 10 pigeon holes, two stationery drawers and a pull-out writing board. The center drawer is a full 24″ wide. The tambour comes fully assembled.

·1·

Table Top Organizer
Craftsman's Corner
Size: 6½″ × 18″ × 15″
Pieces: 22
Time: 2½ hours
Wood: Oak
Item No.: 1CC132
Price: $48.95
Freight: $6.00

If you've no room for a desk, try this handy solution. Oak buttons are included for that pegged look.

·2·

Colonial Style Magazine Rack
Craftsman's Corner
Size: 11″ × 18½″ × 17″
Pieces: 14
Time: 2½ hours
Wood: Oak
Item No.: 1CC130
Price: $49.95
Freight: $6.00

·3·

Two-Drawer File Cabinet
Craftsman's Corner
Size: 26¼″ × 20½″ × 30¾″
Pieces: 62
Time: 6 hours
Wood: Oak
Item No.: 1CC103
Price: $209.95
Freight: $25.00

·4·

Three-Drawer File Cabinet
Craftsman's Corner
Size: 26¼″ × 20½″ × 42½″
Pieces: 75
Time: 8 hours
Wood: Oak
Item No.: 1CC102
Price: $289.95
Freight: $32.00

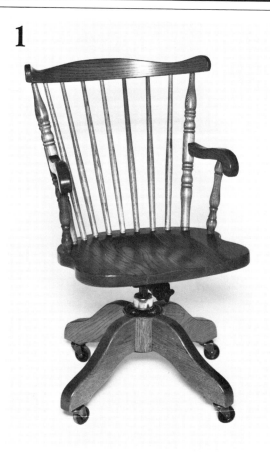

·1·

Duxbury Desk Chair
Zimmerman Chair Shop
Size: 17½" × 20" × 36"
Pieces: 19
Time: 3 hours
Wood: Oak
Item No.: 1ZC101
Price: $195.00
Freight: $11.70

This classic desk chair swivels, adjusts up or down and tilts back. The tension control can be adjusted to accomodate any weight person. Comes complete with casters.

·2·

Bank of England Swivel Chair
Craftsman's Corner
Size: 24" × 23"
(Height is adjustable)
Pieces: KD
Wood: Oak
Item No.: 1CC104
Price: $219.95
Freight: FC

All you need to do is add the protective bumper guard to the seat and set the casters, then finish this comfortable chair patterned after furniture first used in the Bank of England.

·1·

Three-Shelf Master Piece Bookcase
American Forest Products
Size: $10^{11}/_{16}'' \times 35'' \times 41^{3}/_{4}''$
Pieces: 19
Time: $1^{1}/_{4}$ hours
Wood: Pine
Item No.: 1AF105
Price: $81.00
Freight: $10.25

·2·

Barrister Bookshelves
Craftsman's Corner
Size: $13^{3}/_{4}'' \times 36'' \times 49^{1}/_{2}''$
Pieces: 120
Time: 8 hours
Wood: Oak
Item No.: 1CC111
Price: $299.80
Freight: $39.50

Classic stacking bookshelves have become rather difficult to find, but now you can build your own. Glass doors slide up and down just like the originals. All glass and hardware are included.

·3·

Jefferson Bookcase
Craftsman's Corner
Size: $12'' \times 34'' \times 40''$
Pieces: 54
Time: 6 hours
Wood: Oak
Item No.: 1CC115
Price: $149.95
Freight: $18.50

This functional piece which includes both drawers and bookshelves will be a welcome addition to any room. All hardware is included.

·CLOCKS·

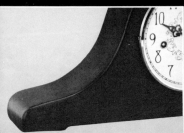

These stately grandfather clocks feature the Moving Moon face of solid brass which shows the phases of the moon above the dial. The solid brass works, crafted in the Black Forest, is a 7-day movement. Although the lyre pendulum is pictured, the more traditional bob pendulum is included. No glass is included.

·1·

Grandfather Clock

Viking Clock Company
Size: 13″ × 20″ × 83″
Pieces: 100
Time: 40 hours
Wood: Oak
Item No.: 1VC101
Price: $607.00
Freight: UPSC

Wood: Cherry
Item No.: 1VC201
Price: $678.00
Freight: UPSC

Wood: Walnut
Item No.: 1VC301
Price: $784.00
Freight: UPSC

·2·

Grandfather Clock

Viking Clock Company
Size: 10″ × 16″ × 75″
Pieces: 85
Time: 35 hours
Wood: Oak
Item No.: 1VC100
Price: $375.00
Freight: UPSC

Wood: Cherry
Item No.: 1VC200
Price: $436.00
Freight: UPSC

Wood: Walnut
Item No.: 1VC300
Price: $476.00
Freight: UPSC

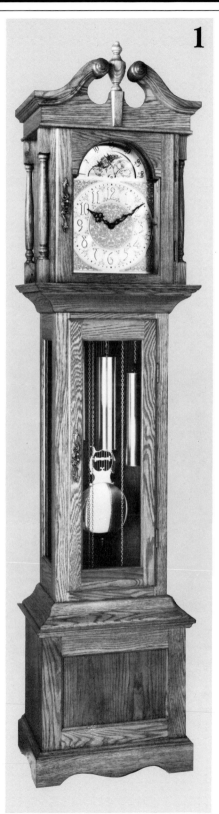

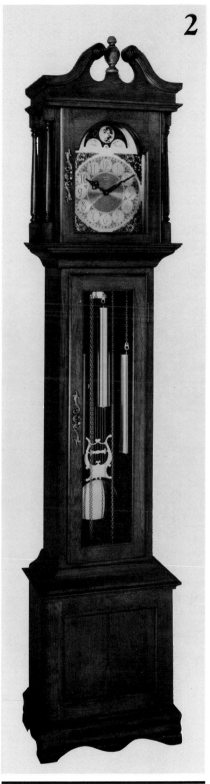

·1·

English Carriage Clock
Viking Clock Company
Size: 5¹/₂″ × 14″ × 15¹/₂″
Pieces: 14
Time: 6 hours
Wood: Walnut
Movement: Electric
Item No.: 1VC102
Price: $196.00
Freight: UPSC

Movement: Brass
Item No.: 1VC202
Price: $196.00
Freight: UPSC

Four chime melodies or silence can be selected. Glass is not included.

·2·

Victorian Teardrop Clock
Viking Clock Company
Size: 5¹/₂″ × 13″ × 23¹/₂″
Pieces: 13
Time: 6 hours
Wood: Walnut
Item No.: 1VC104
Price: $198.00
Freight: UPSC

Pre-assembled door is silk-screened in gold. The 8-day, brass movement strikes both the hour and the half-hour.

·3·

Camelback Clock
Viking Clock Company
Size: 3″ × 20″ × 90″
Pieces: 4
Time: 3 hours
Wood: Honduras Mahogany
Item No.: 1VC106
Price: $127.00
Freight: UPSC

Westminster chimes mark the passing of each quarter-hour and count the hours.

·1·

Railroad Regulator Clock

Viking Clock Company
Size: 4¹/8″ × 13″ × 26″
Pieces: 15
Time: 6 hours
Wood: Oak
Item No.: 1VC107
Price: $129.00
Freight: UPSC

Wood: Cherry
Item No.: 1VC207
Price: $149.00
Freight: UPSC

The silk-screened door glass accents this reproduction with its brass movement and Bim-Bam chimes.

·2·

Bavarian Regulator Clock

Viking Clock Company
Size: 8″ × 14″ × 36″
Pieces: 15
Time: 6 hours
Wood: Walnut
Item No.: 1VC105
Price: $239.00
Freight: UPSC

Solid brass, 14-day movement counts the hours and strikes the half-hours. Glass is not included.

·3·

Schoolhouse Clock

Viking Clock Company
Size: 4″ × 23″ × 14¹/2″
Pieces: 10
Time: 6 hours
Wood: Oak
Item No.: 1VC103
Price: $129.00
Freight: UPSC

Just like the one-room school clock, this clock chimes the half-hour and strikes the hour. The brass and curved glass bezel are included, but the other glass is not.

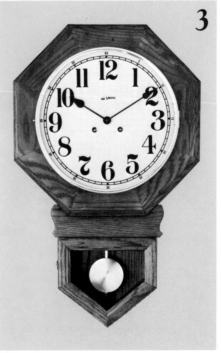

·ENTERTAINMENT·

·1·

Dulcimer
Craftsman's Corner
Size: 7″ × 36″ × 3½″
Pieces: 10 plus hardware
Time: 3 hours
Wood: Walnut
Item No.: 1CC117
Price: $59.95
Freight: $4.00

This unique kit includes tuning pegs, strings, fret bars plus brief history, tuning suggestions, how-to-play instructions and simple tunes to play.

·2·

Music Box
Craftsman's Corner
Size: 8¾″ × 10¾″ × 6¾″
Pieces: 22
Time: 1 hour
Wood: Oak
Item No.: 1CC109
Price: $144.95
Freight: $4.50

Each of these lovely music boxes comes with a Thorens Swiss 30-note movement, etched glass, hardware, velour lining, plus five discs . . . *Lara's Theme, Try to Remember, Moon River, More* and *Edelweiss.*

·3·

Treasure Chest Music Box
Craftsman's Corner
Size: 8½″ × 9½″ × 4½″
Pieces: 14
Time: 1 hour
Wood: Oak
Item No.: 1CC112
Price: $139.95
Freight: $4.00

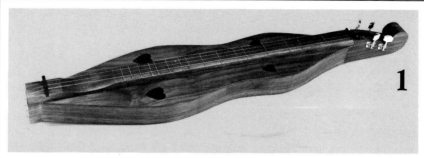

Arrange your entertainment components and records any way you want with these contemporary units from American Forest Products. Each is constructed from extra thick cut Western pine.

·1·

Audio "L"
American Forest Products
Size: 16″ × 53³/₁₆″ × 35¹/₂″
Pieces: 8
Time: ¹/₂ hour
Wood: Pine
Item No.: 1AF114
Price: $170.00
Freight: FC

·2·

Audio Console
American Forest Products
Size: 16″ × 43¹/₄″ × 28″
Pieces: 7
Time: ¹/₂ hour
Wood: Pine
Item No.: 1AF113
Price: $147.50
Freight: FC

·3·

Audio Tower
American Forest Products
Size: 16″ × 22¹/₄″ × 35¹/₂″
Pieces: 6
Time: ¹/₂ hour
Wood: Pine
Item No.: 1AF112
Price: $115.00
Freight: $16.00

·4·

Family Entertainment Center

Craftsman's Corner
Size: 19″ × 31½″ × 63″
Pieces: 89
Time: 10 hours
Wood: Oak
Item No.: 1CC113
Price: $349.95
Freight: $38.00

This family entertainment center is as sturdy as only solid oak and oak veneer construction can be. The television area measures 18″ × 28½″ × 18½″. Upper unit storage areas are each 15½″ deep by 15½″ high and are divided into 19½″ and 8″ widths. The bottom storage area includes a heavy-duty pull-out shelf, designed for a stereo unit which features stops, and a ledge for safety. This area is 15″ × 25″ × 9¼″; the lower area is 18″ × 28½″ × 8½″.

This attractive stacking wine rack is ideal for storing wine bottles and glasses. The starter unit has a ³/₄″ thick top for serving snacks. Each interlocking unit holds eight bottles. The starter unit holds up to twelve stemware glasses and four wine bottles. The unit pictured is composed of one starter unit and four add-on units.

·1·

Wine Rack Starter Unit
Smith Wood Products
Size: 10″ × 22″ × 14″
Pieces: 28
Time: ³/₄ hour
Wood: Oak
Item No.: 1BG101
Price: $44.00
Freight: $4.75

Wine Rack Add-on Unit
Smith Wood Products
Size: 10″ × 20″ × 11″
Pieces: 22
Time: ¹/₂ hour
Wood: Oak
Item No.: 1BG102
Price: $27.00
Freight: $3.50

·2·

Oakie Serving Cart
Smith Wood Products
Size: 19″ × 24″ × 32″
Pieces: 49
Time: 2¹/₂ hours
Wood: Oak
Item No.: 1BG103
Price: $145.00
Freight: $10.50

This handy serving cart features a slatted storage shelf, stemware rack and combination storage drawer/serving tray. The 1¹/₂″ thick top can be used for work space, or for holding microwave units. Casters provide easy mobility.

·WALL SYSTEMS·

This modular system of shelves, storage and desk units is composed of six units which have interlocking parts for strength plus brushed metal drawer and door pulls for the finishing touch. The possibilities are endless and pieces can be added at any time, just use your imagination. Be sure to order a base unit for each piece that will sit on the floor.

·1·

Design Line Two-Door Case
American Forest Products
Size: 16″ × 26″ × 6½″
Pieces: 15
Time: ¾ hour
Wood: Pine
Item No.: 1AF121
Price: $105.00
Freight: $10.25

·2·

Design Line Base
American Forest Products
Size: 15″ × 26″ × 3½″
Pieces: 4
Time: 5 minutes
Wood: Pine
Item No.: 1AF118
Price: $13.25
Freight: $2.50

·3·

Design Line Two-Shelf Case
American Forest Products
Size: 15¼″ × 26″ × 26½″
Pieces: 13
Time: ½ hour
Wood: Pine
Item No.: 1AF119
Price: $76.25
Freight: $8.50

·4·

Design Line
Drop-Lid Case
American Forest Products
Size: 16″ × 26″ × 26½″
Pieces: 14
Time: ¾ hour
Wood: Pine
Item No.: 1AF120
Price: $94.50
Freight: $9.50

·5·

Design Line
Three-Drawer Case
American Forest Products
Size: 15⅞″ × 26″ × 26½″
Pieces: 26
Time: ¾ hour
Wood: Pine
Item No.: 1AF122
Price: $102.50
Freight: $13.00

·6·

Design Line Desk Bridge
American Forest Products
Size: 15⅞″ × 26″ × 5½″
Pieces: 12
Time: ¼ hour
Wood: Pine
Item No.: 1AF123
Price: $26.25
Freight: $4.00

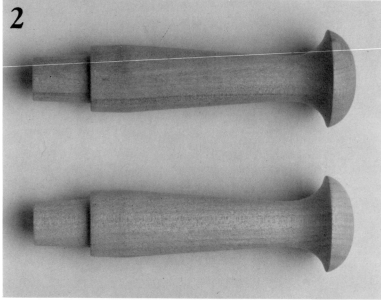

Unusual yet practical are these Shaker pegboard systems for out-of-the-way storage of everything from chairs to dried herbs. Those pictured are made precisely like those in the 1830 Brick Dwelling at Hancock Shaker Village. They are 3½″ wide clear pine with beaded edges. Each pegboard comes with two pegs per foot of board, or add as many pegs as you like by ordering them in any quantity. Each peg is 3½″ long with a ⅝″ long tapered tenon.

·1·

24″ Shaker Pegboard
Shaker Workshops
Item No.: 1SW136
Price: $8.50
Freight: PP

36″ Shaker Pegboard
Item No.: 1SW137
Price: $11.25
Freight: PP

48″ Shaker Pegboard
Item No.: 1SW138
Price: $14.00
Freight: PP

·2·

Maple Shaker Pegs
Shaker Workshops
Quantity: 10
Item No.: 1SW133
Price: $3.40
Freight: PP

Quantity: 50
Item No.: 1SW134
Price: $11.50
Freight: PP

Quantity: 100
Item No.: 1SW135
Price: $21.50
Freight: PP

Quantity: 500
Item No.: 1SW139
Price: $102.60
Freight: PP

Choose from these Shaker designs to make your pegboard even more authentic. Each is uniquely functional and decorative in any setting from the kitchen to the bathroom . . . or even at the office.

·3·

Hanging Shelves

Shaker Workshops
Size: 7″ × 27″ × 25″
Pieces: 5
Time: 3 hours
Wood: Maple
Item No.: 1SW114
Price: $45.00
Freight: $3.25

Shelves are 5″, 6″ and 7″ deep.

·4·

Adjustable Sconce

Shaker Workshops
Size: 8″ × 10″ × 26″
Pieces: 5
Time: 1 hour
Wood: Cherry
Item No.: 1SW112
Price: $23.00
Freight: $2.45

·5·

Hand or Hanging Mirror

Shaker Workshops
Size: 9¼″ long by 4″ wide
Pieces: 3
Time: 1 hour
Wood: Maple
Item No.: 1SW124
Price: $8.75
Freight: $1.45

·SHAKER ACCENTS·

·1·

Towel Rack

Shaker Workshops
Size: 13″ × 33⅞″ × 33½″
Pieces: 8
Time: 3 hours
Wood: Pine
Item No.: 1SW111
Price: $38.75
Freight: $2.75

The unique octagonal rails of this rack are well suited for airing quilts and blankets, hanging towels or drying wet socks and mittens.

·2·

Shoemaker's Candlestand

Shaker Workshops
Size: 6½″ × 16½″
Pieces: 5
Time: 2 hours
Wood: Maple
Item No.: 1SW125
Price: $37.50
Freight: $2.75

This unique candlestand was found in a long-closed cobbler's shop at the Mt. Lebanon Community. The candle platform is 14″ wide and adjusts on the threaded centerpost.

·3·

Spool Stand

Shaker Workshops
Size: 6″ × 5″
Pieces: 3
Time: 2 hours
Wood: Maple
Item No.: 1SW113
Price: $13.75
Freight: $1.70

This reproduction comes with fabric, DMC floss, stuffing material and ten brass pins to be inserted into the base.

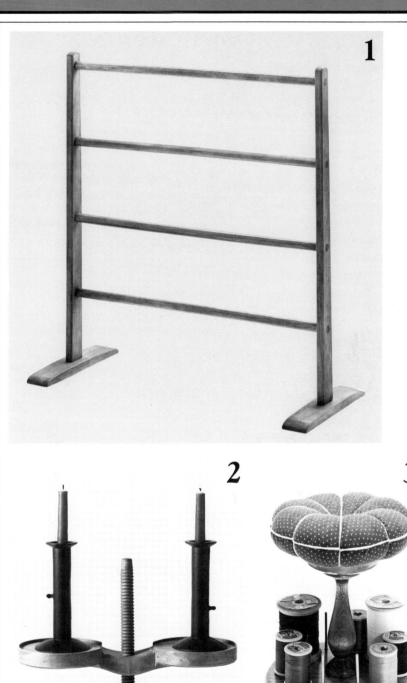

·ORDERING INFORMATION·

Garlinghouse is the clearinghouse for all furniture kit orders from this catalogue. You send your order directly to us; we contact the various manufacturers who then ship your furniture kits directly to you. We're glad to provide this customer service to speed up and simplify your ordering at no added cost.

·1·
Ordering

Be sure to include your complete mailing address and a telephone number where you can be reached during the day, just in case there is some question about your order. We want it taken care of right the first time.

·2·
Shipping

If your order is being shipped freight collect (FC) or United Parcel Service collect (UPSC), you must include your complete street address rather than a post office box number. If no one is at your home during the day, you should include your work address to ensure proper delivery. Specified charges for freight should be remitted with your payment; charges are accurate for the United States only.

·3·
Canadian Orders

Items marked FC and PP will be shipped the same as for U.S. residents. As United Parcel Service does not operate in Canada, items marked UPSC must be sent parcel post. Figure the parcel post rate from Topeka, Kansas and remit that amount as the freight charge. For those items which list a specific dollar amount for freight, double the U.S. rate and remit it with your order.

·4·
Credit Card Orders

MasterCard, Visa, American Express credit cards may be used for orders of $10.00 or more. Be sure to include your credit card number, the expiration date and your signature. Without this information we will not be able to ship the order. You may also use your credit card to order by phone if you wish. Call (913) 267-2490 any weekday between 8:30 and 4:30 and we will be happy to take your credit card order. Have all information ready. No collect calls please.

·5·
Checks

Make all checks and money orders payable to:

The Garlinghouse Company
320 S.W. 33rd Street, P.O. Box 299
Topeka, Kansas 66601-0299

·6·
Guarantee

We have selected quality kits from reputable manufacturers and believe that you will be completely satisfied. If there are any difficulties, contact the manufacturer directly according to the instructions included with your kit. If you do not receive satisfaction, we would like to hear about it so that we can make our own inquiry.

·ORDER FORMS·

Ship To: 19002   **Payment:** ☐ Check ☐ Money Order

Name _____   ☐ MasterCard ☐ Visa ☐ American Express

Street _____ Apt. No. _____   Card No. _____

City _____ State _____ Zip _____   Expiration Date _____

Daytime Phone No. _____   Signature _____

No C.O.D. Orders

Item. No.	Description	Wood	Qnty.	Price	Freight	Total

The Garlinghouse Company   Order Total

320 S.W. 33rd Street, P. O. Box 299   Kansas Residents Add 4% Sales Tax

Topeka, Kansas 66601-0299 (913) 267-2490   Total

Ship To: 19002   **Payment:** ☐ Check ☐ Money Order

Name _____   ☐ MasterCard ☐ Visa ☐ American Express

Street _____ Apt. No. _____   Card No. _____

City _____ State _____ Zip _____   Expiration Date _____

Daytime Phone No. _____   Signature _____

No C.O.D. Orders

Item. No.	Description	Wood	Qnty.	Price	Freight	Total

The Garlinghouse Company   Order Total

320 S.W. 33rd Street, P. O. Box 299   Kansas Residents Add 4% Sales Tax

Topeka, Kansas 66601-0299 (913) 267-2490   Total

Ship To: 19002   **Payment:** ☐ Check ☐ Money Order

Name _____   ☐ MasterCard ☐ Visa ☐ American Express

Street _____ Apt. No. _____   Card No. _____

City _____ State _____ Zip _____   Expiration Date _____

Daytime Phone No. _____   Signature _____

No C.O.D. Orders

Item. No.	Description	Wood	Qnty.	Price	Freight	Total

The Garlinghouse Company   Order Total

320 S.W. 33rd Street, P. O. Box 299   Kansas Residents Add 4% Sales Tax

Topeka, Kansas 66601-0299 (913) 267-2490   Total